My Best Book of
Wolves and Wild Dogs

Christiane Gunzi

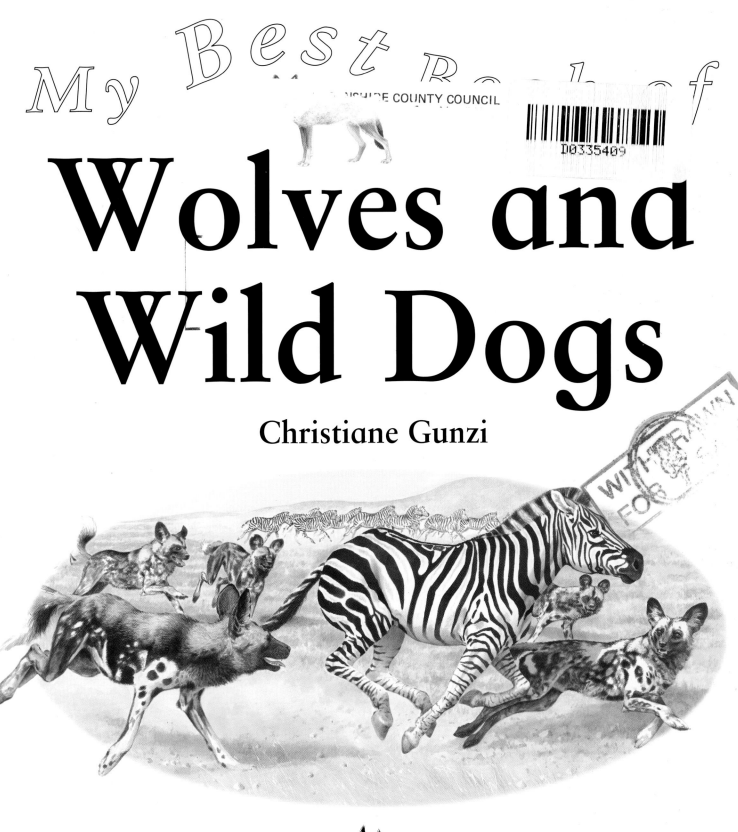

KINGFISHER

Contents

KINGFISHER

Kingfisher Publications Plc,
New Penderel House,
283–288 High Holborn,
London WC1V 7HZ

www.kingfisherpub.com

Created for Kingfisher Publications Plc
by Picthall & Gunzi Limited

Author and editor: Christiane Gunzi
Designer: Dominic Zwemmer
Consultant: Lisa Wallis,
UK Wolf Conservation Trust
Illustrators: Michael Langham Rowe,
William Oliver, John Barber,
Bernard Robinson

First published by Kingfisher
Publications Plc 2003

10 9 8 7 6 5 4 3 2 1

1TR/0103/WKT/MAR(MAR)/128/KMA

Copyright © Kingfisher
Publications Plc 2003

A CIP catalogue record for this book
is available from the British Library.

ISBN 0 7534 0820 1

Printed in Hong Kong

4 Meet
the wolf

6 A world of
wild dogs

14 Finding
food

16 African
hunting dogs

24 Racing
jackals

26 Amazing
wild dogs

8 The first wolves

10 Meeting and greeting

12 Growing up

18 Wild dogs of Australia

20 Mountain dogs

22 Foxes of the desert

28 Wild dogs in danger

30 Studying wolves

31 Glossary

32 Index

Meet the wolf

The grey wolf is the biggest member of the dog family. Grey wolves, maned wolves, red wolves and wild dogs are all meat-eaters, or carnivores. Grey wolves and many other wild dogs live in large groups called packs. Wolves hunt mammals, including moose, caribou and rabbits. Wolves once lived in many parts of the world. Today, they are found in only a few wild places.

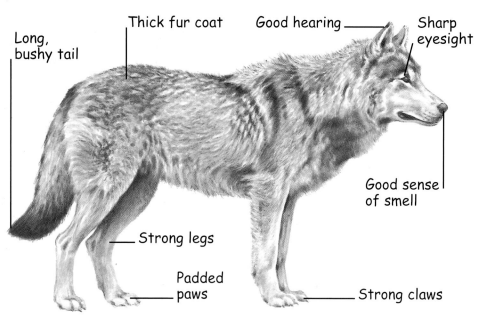

Long, bushy tail

Thick fur coat

Good hearing

Sharp eyesight

Good sense of smell

Strong legs

Padded paws

Strong claws

A grey wolf's body

Grey wolves have white, grey, brown or black fur, and in winter it is very thick. They have padded paws for running, and strong claws and sharp teeth for hunting. Wolves have good sight and hearing, and an excellent sense of smell.

Top dogs

Most packs contain up to ten wolves. The pack leader is either the 'alpha' male or the 'alpha' female. In spring and summer, the wolf pack stays in one place, but in autumn and winter the wolves have to travel a long way to find food.

The alpha male and alpha female greet an older member of the pack.

Young wolves learn to fight by playing.

A world of wild dogs

Wild dogs are mammals that live on every continent except Antarctica. They include wolves, foxes, dingos, dholes, zorros and hunting dogs. All wild dogs belong to the same family, which includes domestic, or pet dogs. Every domestic dog in the world is related to the grey wolf, which has existed for a million years.

Dingo (Australia)
weighs 8.3–21.5kg
72–111cm long

Grey wolf
(North America,
Asia, Europe,
Russia)
weighs 16–60kg
100–150cm long

Dhole (Asia)
weighs 10–20kg
90cm long

Red fox
(North Africa, Asia,
Europe, North America)
weighs 3–11kg
58–90cm long

Red wolf
(North America)
weighs 18–41kg
95–120cm long

Maned wolf
(South America)
weighs 20–23kg
124–132cm long

Coyote
(North America)
weighs 9–16kg
70–97cm long

Bush dog
(South
America)
weighs 5–7kg
57–75cm long

Golden jackal
(Africa, Asia)
weighs 7–15kg
60–106cm long

Summer
coat

Spring
coat

Arctic fox
(Arctic)
weighs 3.5kg
53–55cm long

Winter coat

African
hunting dog
(Africa)
weighs 17–36kg
76–112cm long

A change of coat

In winter, the Arctic fox's coat turns white to
blend with the snow in the frozen Arctic where
it lives. In spring, the fox's fur starts to change
colour. By summer, its coat is dark brown.

7

The first wolves

Dog-like creatures have existed for about 37 million years.

About eight million years ago, a mammal called *Eucyon* lived on the plains of North America. *Eucyon* is the ancestor of all wolves, jackals and coyotes. One of the first wolves was the dire wolf, which lived more than 10,000 years ago. This powerful carnivore probably hunted in packs. Its strong teeth could break the bones of mammoths and other prey.

Woolly mammoth helplessly trapped in sticky tar

Grey wolf's ancestors

Dire wolves were only a little bit smaller than the grey wolves that live in the USA today. *Eucyon* was about the size of a red fox. *Hesperocyon* was even smaller, probably the size of a cat.

Hesperocyon lived about 37 million years ago.

Eucyon lived about 8 million years ago.

Dire wolf lived over 10,000 years ago.

Dire wolves in danger

Dire wolves roamed North America at the same time as mammoths. In ancient tar pits in Rancho La Brea, USA, scientists have found thousands of dire wolf bones. The animals became trapped in the sticky tar pits and died there.

Hungry dire wolves, tempted by the trapped prey, stand on the edge of the tar pit where they will become trapped themselves.

Meeting and greeting

Wolves communicate with their bodies, their faces and by making different noises.

The alpha male and alpha female are in charge of the rest of the pack. They hold their tails up high to show other wolves how important they are. Less important members of the pack crouch with their tails between their legs to greet their pack leaders.

Happy   Playful

Frightened   Angry

A wolf's moods

Wolves make faces to show how they are feeling. A happy wolf has its ears up. A frightened wolf has its ears flat. A playful wolf looks as if it is smiling. An angry wolf shows its fangs.

Alpha female being greeted by a less important female

Call of the coyote

Coyotes and wolves howl to tell other pack members where they are, or to show rivals exactly where their territory is. Coyotes look like wolves but they are smaller.

Coyote howling at dusk

A place in the pack

In the pack, every wolf has its own place, or rank. This means that some wolves are more important than others. The alpha pair are the only two that have young.

A young wolf greets the alpha male by touching noses.

Growing up

The red fox is a handsome creature which has reddish-orange fur and a long, bushy tail. Red foxes are found all over the world, particularly in Europe, Australia and the USA. They live in many different habitats, such as woodlands, deserts, farms and cities. The grey fox is found only in North, Central and South America. It likes to live in woodlands and it can climb trees like a cat!

Grey foxes

1 A female grey fox gives birth to about four young in spring or summer, in a den under a tree or log.

2 For the first few weeks the female feeds her young on milk. Then the male brings food to the family inside the den.

3 For four months, the cubs stay with their mother, close to the den. She teaches them how to hunt for birds and small mammals such as mice.

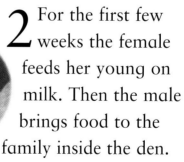

4 After four months, a young grey fox begins to find its own food. It hunts for prey, and climbs trees to feed on fruit, such as wild cherries and grapes.

A fox's den is called an 'earth'.

Happy families

A red fox usually has four or five cubs, and they are very playful. At two months old, red fox cubs start to eat earthworms, beetles, small mammals, birds and fruit. Foxes like to bury their spare food, and they usually remember where they hid it!

The female red fox, or vixen, guards her cubs while they play.

13

Finding food

 **Most wild dogs, including wolves, are known as carnivores because they hunt and eat other animals.** Some wild dogs, such as foxes and jackals, are called omnivores. This is because they hunt prey, but also feed on fruit, plants, birds' eggs, carrion and food in rubbish bins. When wild dogs search for food it is usually at night, or in the early morning or evening.

Dingos chase a grey kangaroo at night.

Dingos in the dark

Dingos are the biggest predators in Australia. They usually hunt at night, alone or in pairs. Dingos feed on rabbits and other mammals.

Rubbish raiders

Jackals and foxes often live
near towns and close to
people. In the early morning
and at dusk, these clever
wild dogs scavenge for
leftover food in piles of
rubbish. Jackals are
very daring!

15

African hunting dogs

These colourful wild dogs live in packs on the African grasslands, where they hunt gazelle, antelope, zebra, impala and wildebeest. Hunting dogs never stay in the same place for more than two or three days. They wander over huge areas and travel hundreds of kilometres. These dogs look after each other. After a hunt they bring food to the sick, injured and older members of the pack that stayed behind.

Baby-sitting

Pups stay in a den for the first four weeks. Once the pups leave the den, other adults look after them when their mother goes hunting.

The big chase

Hunting dogs look for prey in the mornings and evenings, when it is cool. They hunt well together and can run at up to 55km/h. One dog leads the pack and they may chase an animal for several kilometres.

The pattern on every dog's coat is different.

A friendly pack

There are usually 10 to 15 African hunting dogs in a pack. Unlike some wild dogs, these are friendly towards each other and do not fight often. During the hottest part of the day they sleep and rest in the shade. When it is time to go hunting, they wake up, stretch and greet each other with great excitement.

Pack of African hunting dogs resting

African hunting dogs hunting a zebra

Wild dogs of Australia

Dingos are wild dogs that live in Australia, but they were not always wild. Thousands of years ago, people travelling from Asia to Australia took some domestic dogs with them. Eventually, these dogs began to live in the wild. In some parts of Australia, dingos are a nuisance to sheep farmers because they kill and eat sheep. To keep dingos away from the sheep there is a fence 5,000km long across Australia!

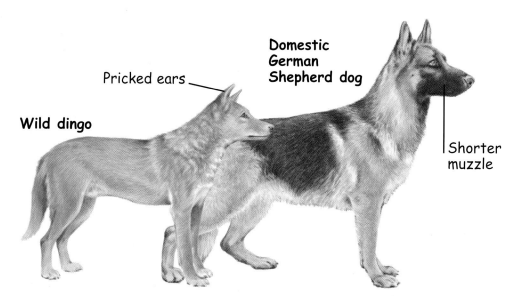

Pricked ears

Domestic German Shepherd dog

Wild dingo

Shorter muzzle

Dingos and domestic dogs

Dingos belong to the same species as domestic dogs such as German Shepherds. A dingo looks similar to a German Shepherd, but it is smaller, with a longer muzzle. A dingo's ears are always upright, or pricked.

The orange colour of a dingo's coat helps it to blend in with its sandy habitat.

Family of dingos drinking at a water-hole

A daily drink of water

Dingos live in family groups and the young stay with their parents for up to three years. These wild dogs need to drink every day, so they usually live near water. They cannot bark, but they howl to communicate with each other.

Mountain dogs

High in the mountains of Asia there are dogs called dholes. These wild dogs have existed for millions of years. Dholes prefer to live in forest areas, but they are also found on open plains. They are usually seen in packs of about ten animals. Dholes like water and are very good at swimming. After eating, they often go to drink at a pool or to sit in the water.

A dhole has a bushy tail, which it can wag, just like a domestic dog.

A dhole's diet

Dholes are different from all other dogs because they have 42 teeth instead of 44. They eat all kinds of food, from large mammals such as guar and caribou, to lizards, goats and hares, and even berries.

Guar

Caribou

Wild boar

Wild goat

Hare

Berries

Lizard

Dholes call to each other by making a whistling sound. They also mew, and cluck like a chicken!

All together now

Dholes usually work together when they hunt fierce and dangerous prey, such as wild boar. Dholes also work together to care for their young. The adults in a pack help to feed and guard all the pups.

Foxes of the desert

Some foxes live in hot, dry deserts. Their large ears help to keep them cool. To hide from the heat of the sun, they dig a burrow in the sand. There is not much water in a desert. Some foxes get enough water from their food, so they never need to drink. An Arctic fox spends its life in a cold desert. Thick fur keeps this fox warm and camouflages it as it hunts on the snow.

Fennec fox

These foxes eat lizards, eggs, rodents, insects and plants. They are active mainly at night, and stay in a burrow during the day.

Fox types

There are at least 14 kinds of fox and they are all different colours and sizes. The red fox is the largest, and the fennec fox (24–41cm long) is the smallest.

Red fox
58-90cm long

Grey fox
53-81cm long

Kit fox
37-53cm long

Ruppell's fox
40-52cm long

Bengal fox
45-60cm long

Arctic fox
53-55cm long

Pampas fox
up to 65cm long

Bat-eared fox

The huge ears of a bat-eared fox help it to listen for beetles, termites, spiders and scorpions. It has sharp claws for digging, and up to 50 small teeth for crunching tiny creatures.

The fox's ears can be up to 10cm long.

A bat-eared fox shows her young how to pounce on a scorpion.

Racing jackals

With long, muscular legs and a lightweight body, a jackal is built for speed. Golden jackals live in open countryside in parts of Africa, southeast Europe and south Asia. Black-backed and side-striped jackals are found only on the African savannah. In some areas jackals are hunted by people. It is important to protect jackals and their natural habitats so that they continue to survive in the wild.

Moving home

The side-striped jackal gives birth to up to four young in a den. If there is any sign of danger, the female moves all the young to a new den.

Jackals with black backs

Black-backed jackals often hunt in pairs, which makes it easier for them to catch prey. They eat small mammals, insects and plants. Black-backed jackals also scavenge on carrion, or the remains of prey, left by lions.

Hungry jackal

Jackals are omnivores, so they eat insects, birds, reptiles, amphibians, plants and mammals, as well as carrion. If there is too much food to eat, a golden jackal hides any leftovers under a plant, or digs a hole and buries the food. The golden jackal returns to its hidden store of food later, when it is hungry.

Golden jackal burying a bird

Pair of black-backed jackals hunting for food at night

25

Lion's mane

A maned wolf has thick hair around its shoulders, almost like a lion's mane. It stalks mammals, birds and other animals in the long grass, and pounces on its prey like a fox.

A maned wolf can leap high over long grass.

A type of wild guinea pig, called a cavy, hiding in the grass

Amazing wild dogs

The tallest wild dog is found in South America and is called the maned wolf. Maned wolves are 87cm high at the shoulder. They live in grasslands, savannah and at the edge of forests. Each year, the grasslands where they live are burned, so these dogs are endangered. The South American bush dog looks more like a bear cub than a wild dog, but it is a dog. Bush dogs live in rainforests and at the edges of savannah, close to water. They can swim well.

Bush dogs leaving their underground burrow

Burrowing bush dogs

These carnivores live in burrows in groups of up to eight animals. They have long, strong claws for digging. Bush dogs are good hunters and catch animals bigger than themselves, such as deer and large rodents.

Wild dogs in danger

The main threat to wild dogs is from humans. For hundreds of years, wolves and wild dogs have been hunted by people for their fur and meat, and because they sometimes kill and eat farm animals. Today, many wild dogs are endangered. Some, such as the African hunting dog and the Ethiopian wolf, may soon be extinct. If these animals are to survive in the wild, we must protect them and their habitats.

Wolves of Africa

The Ethiopian wolf lives on grasslands high in the mountains of Ethiopia, in Africa, where it hunts for mole rats and other rodents. This wolf is so rare that there are only a few hundred left in the wild.

Family of Ethiopian wolves playing

Fake fur, not fox fur!

Thousands of foxes and wolves have been killed so that people can wear fur. Now there are fake furs that people can wear instead. They look very like real fur.

Small-eared zorro

This wild dog is a kind of South American fox
that lives in rainforests. It is an endangered animal
because many trees in the forests where it lives are
being cut down and burned. Parts of the rainforest are
being cleared to make room for buildings and farms.

Clearing where
rainforest trees are
being cut down to make
way for farmland

A small-eared
zorro in its
rainforest home

Studying wolves

There are only a few thousand wild wolves left in some parts of the world. The red wolf was hunted so much that it almost became extinct. Scientists saved the red wolf by breeding a few in captivity. In national parks in North America, red wolves are being released into the wild. Today there are between 50 and 80 red wolves successfully living in these parks.

Releasing red wolves

When red wolves are released into the wild, they wear collars with radio transmitters on them. These transmitters send out signals so that scientists can keep track of the wolves.

Tracking grey wolves

In the cold forests in the far north of America, experts follow packs of grey wolves by aeroplane. They check that the animals are well, and make sure that they have enough prey to eat.

A herd of caribou makes good prey for wolves.

Scientists following grey wolves in an aeroplane

Glossary

alpha The first letter of the Greek alphabet. This word is used to describe the male and female leaders of a wolf pack.

camouflage The different colours and markings on an animal that help it to hide in the wild.

captivity An animal that has been caught and is not free is in captivity.

carnivore An animal, such as a cat or dog, that eats meat.

carrion An animal that has been killed, but is not yet completely eaten by its predator. Other animals often eat the remains.

communicate Animals communicate, or talk to each other, by smell, by voice, or by the way that they stand or move.

continents Huge areas of land. There are seven continents: Asia, Africa, North America, South America, Europe, Australia and Antarctica.

domestic Not wild. An animal, such as a dog or cat, that lives with people, is said to be domestic.

endangered An animal or plant that is in danger of dying out forever. Maned wolves are endangered animals.

extinct An animal or plant that has died out forever. Dire wolves and woolly mammoths are extinct animals.

habitat An animal's habitat is its natural home in the wild. A grey fox's natural habitat is woodland.

mammals Animals, such as dogs and cats, that are covered with fur or hair, give birth to live young and feed them milk.

mane An area of thick fur around a lion's shoulders. Maned wolves also have a type of mane.

omnivore An animal, such as a fox, jackal or bear, that eats fruit, plants and eggs, as well as meat.

pack A large group of wolves or wild dogs is known as a pack. There may be dozens of animals in one pack.

predators Animals that hunt and prey on other animals are known as predators. Wolves and lions are predators.

prey Animals that are hunted and eaten by wolves and other predators.

rodents Small mammals such as rats, mice and squirrels, are rodents. They are prey for wild dogs.

savannah Huge, flat areas of grassland in Africa, with only a few trees. African hunting dogs live on the savannah.

scavengers Animals that search for and finish off food left by other animals. Jackals are scavengers.

territory The area where an animal lives is called its territory. Wolves have large territories.

Index

A
African hunting dog 7, 16–17, 28
ancient wild dogs 8, 9, 20
Arctic fox 7, 22

B
bat-eared fox 23
Bengal fox 22
black-backed jackal 24, 25
body language 10
breeding 11, 12, 13, 24, 30
bush dog 7, 27

C
camouflage 22, 31
carnivores 4, 27, 31
claws 4, 23, 27
climbing 12
communication 10–11, 21, 31
coyote 7, 11
cubs 12, 13

D
dens (burrows) 12, 16, 22, 24, 27
dhole 6, 20
dingo 6, 14, 18–19
dire wolf 8, 9
dog family 4
domestic dog 6, 18, 31

E
ears 10, 22, 23
endangered wild dogs 27, 28–29, 31

Ethiopian wolf 28
expressions 10
extinction 28, 30, 31
eyesight 4

F
fangs 10
fennec fox 22
fighting 5, 17
food 4, 16–17, 21, 22, 24, 26
fox 6, 12–13, 22–23
fur 4, 7, 22, 28

G
German Shepherd 18
golden jackal 7, 24
grey fox 12, 22
grey wolf 4, 6, 9, 30

H
hearing 4
homes, loss of 27, 29
howling 11
hunting 4, 16, 21, 24, 26, 27
hunting dogs 6, 7, 16–17

J
jackals 7, 15, 24–25

K
kit fox 22

L
legs 4, 24

M
maned wolf 4, 7, 26, 31

P
pack leaders 4–5, 10–11
packs 4, 5, 10, 11, 16, 17, 20, 31
pampas fox 22
paws 4, 22
prey 4, 16, 21, 22, 23, 24, 26
pups 16, 21

R
radio transmitter 30
red fox 6, 12, 13, 22
red wolf 4, 6, 30
Ruppell's fox 22

S
side-striped jackal 24

T
tail 4, 10, 20
teeth 4, 10, 21
territory 11, 31

W
water 19, 20, 22, 27
wolf pack 4, 5, 10, 11, 30, 31
wolves 4, 6, 8–9, 10, 11, 27, 28, 30

Y
young 11, 12, 16, 21, 24, 31

Z
zorro 6, 29